Yes, We Can Win Men For Christ

By

Pastor Zachary N. Hicks

Yes, We Can Win Men For Christ

COPYRIGHT 2004 BY Zachary N. Hicks

First Edition 2004

All rights reserved.

Reproduction of text in whole or in part without the express written consent by the author is not permitted and is unlawful according to the 1976 U. S. Copyright Act.

Scripture quotations have been taken from the King James Version of the Bible.

To Contact the Author:

Pastor Zachary N. Hicks

Faith Clinic Church of God in Christ

12260 Camden, Detroit, Michigan 48213

(313) 372-3429 * www.FaithClinic.org

Published by:

Cyberlab Publishing

P O Box 618

Dimondale, Michigan 48821

www.cyberlabpublishing.com

Yes, We Can Win Men For Christ/Zachary N. Hicks
ISBN # 0-9746501-3-7

Contents

Dedication	4
Introduction	5
Chapter 1 We Are Workers With God	7
Chapter 2 Building Upon Christ's Foundation	13
Chapter 3 Having the Right Equipment for the Job	19
Chapter 4 Love Constrains Us to Pray and Act	27
Chapter 5 Reaping the Harvest	35
Chapter 6 Renewing the Minds of Men	41
Chapter 7 Nurturing Spiritual Babies, but Men	47
Chapter 8 Preparing Men for the Harvest	53
Chapter 9 Men that Overcame	57
Chapter 10 Summary	63

Dedication

This book is dedicated to the late Superintendent Edgar H. Hicks and Mother Easter V. Hicks, my mother and father who taught me the things of Christ. Also, to my wife, Evangelist Lisa M. Hicks, who has truly been an inspiration to me for over 25 years. To my cousin and spiritual mother, Evangelist Verna Brookins of Peabody, Massachusetts, who has been a mentor to me and my wife and who has always been there for us. Last but certainly not least to Bishop P. A. Brooks who has always encouraged and shown faith in me. Thank you for being a mentor.

Special Thanks

To Sister Onnie Jacque, for her tirelessness, willingness and unrivaled dedication in the preparation and completion of the manuscript. To Deacon Shawn Jacque for going the extra mile. To Senior Associate Pastor Dennis and Evangelist Jacqueline Fair, for continuously encouraging me to write. To Missionary Nina Batie, for her contribution in the completion of this book. I would also like to thank all of my family, and the members of Faith Clinic Church of God in Christ for their love and support.

Introduction

In this book "Yes, We Can Win Men for Christ", we can clearly see how one local church, Faith Clinic Church of God in Christ, under the leadership of Pastor Zachary Hicks has consistently won men to Christ. Pastor Zachary Hicks has developed the Faith Clinic family into a growing ministry, with over 12 years of ministering to men in Detroit, Michigan. He has established a vibrant men's ministry that has led many men to Jesus Christ.

His goal is to win one million men to the Lord, and with his motto "win the lost at all cost", we believe he can achieve it. Through its Men's Shelter, City-Wide Outreach Ministry, Street Walking Ministry, Men Ministering to Men Ministry, and other ministries geared towards witnessing to men, Faith Clinic has touched the lives of thousands of men, winning a great many of them for Christ. God has blessed them to draw men from all walks of life into His Kingdom.

It is without doubt, that Pastor Zachary Hicks has a mandate to minister to men. He believes "the devil works on men overtime in his attempt to keep them in bondage and out of their rightful place as the leaders of their households. When a man is in his God-assigned position as the head of his family, things, for the most part fall into place. "Yes, We Can Win Men for Christ" demonstrates unequivocally that individually and collectively we can win men to Christ.

CHAPTER I

We Are Workers With God

Jesus' words to Peter and Andrew as He walked by their fishing boat were, "**Follow me and I will make you fishers of men**". (**Matthew 2: 19**) Even today, Jesus is saying to those that believe on Him, follow me and I will make you fishers of men. As we follow Christ, we should yield ourselves more to Him, so that He can use us to accomplish great things for His Kingdom.

Believers must be followers of Christ

It is imperative that we understand that if we do not follow Him, we cannot expect to win men to Christ. The word "follow" means to imitate or to copy after. Jesus said, "**Take my yoke upon you and learn of me**". (**Matthew 11:29**) Therefore, it stands to reason that every follower should learn about Christ to the extent that they can imitate or copy His life and ministry. There is a distinct difference between knowing about Jesus, and actually knowing Him. Those that know Him have taken the time to develop a relationship with Him after they knew about Him. Consequently, they become more like Christ, imitating His life, and developing a confidence in God that gives them peace within.

1 Corinthians 3:9 states, "**For we are laborers together with God, ye are God's husbandry, ye are God's building**." As a result of our relationship with Christ, our desire is to please Him by doing His will. It should be understood that we are Christ's witnesses in the earth. We are appointed to represent Him as ambassadors with power and authority. He told us to pray to the Father, that He will send more laborers to reap the harvest. Therefore, every believer should be committed to harvesting the world and bringing others to Jesus. There is room for everyone who is willing to labor, to see their family members, friends, co-workers, and even strangers come into the Kingdom of God.

It is no coincidence that the scripture declares; "**For we are**

laborers together with God . . ." The business of reconciling men to God through Christ is God's business. We, as laborers with God, have to be sure that we are following His instructions. We follow His instructions through the leading of the Holy Ghost, and by obeying the Bible, which is the word of God. It is through the word that we learn that God commanded us to go all over the world and preach the gospel. He also told us to go into the vineyard and work.

Believers are the Light that Christ will use

Through His word, we learn that **"We are the light of the world. A city that is set on a hill cannot be hid."** (**Matthew 5: 14**) The scripture states that we are God's husbandry and building. We make up the Kingdom of God in the earth. If men are going to enter the Kingdom of God, we that are in the Kingdom will have to go and get those who are still outside of the Kingdom. In **St. John Chapter 1**, the scripture demonstrates a mathematical principle for building the Kingdom of God. Two men heard Jesus speaking and wanted to know where He lived. One of the men that followed Him was Andrew.

After hearing Jesus, Andrew then found his brother and brought him to Christ. The next day Jesus found Philip. Philip then found Nathanael and brought him to Christ. Within two days the number of people following Jesus grew to five. For men to come into the Kingdom of God, someone will have to invite them.

Any man that does not know Jesus is spiritually lost and desperately needs to be found. Sometimes, God will send men to us as He did with Peter, in **Acts 10: 19-20,** and other times God will send us to them, as He did with Philip in **Acts: 29**. As workers with God, we must always be ready to do our job, following the Master's instructions closely. Peter and Philip were successful in reaping the harvest, and we can be just as successful.

God can use you to lead others to Christ

There was a young man named **Michael** that I used to work with, who became my friend. At some point Michael became addicted to cocaine, which lead to the loss of his job and family. He was so strung out that he was living in abandoned buildings. Through hanging with the wrong crowd Michael became tough, hardheaded and stubborn. As the Lord led my wife and I, we witnessed to Michael, by sharing both God's love and our concern for him. We left him cooked food at the bottom of the stairs of the abandoned building in which he was living. At the bottom of the bag, in which we had placed his food, we would place a gospel track that he might read. Over time with much prayer and fasting, and being persistent in showing loving kindness on our part, Michael accepted the invitation to come to Christ. Like Peter and Philip, we reaped our harvest, and like Andrew and Philip we found Michael and brought him to Jesus. Today Michael is working in ministry and inviting others to know Christ.

When we are leading others to Christ, we have to be mindful of **Jeremiah 31:3**, which says, "**. . . I have loved thee with an everlasting love: therefore with lovingkindness have I drawn thee.**" It is God's will for us to love and show kindness continually to those that we are leading to Christ.

Yes, We Can Win Men For Christ / Zachary N. Hicks

CHAPTER II

Building Upon Christ's Foundation

There was a man named **Bernard** who just wandered the streets of Detroit. Originally from Chicago, Illinois, he had come to Detroit to be with his brother. However, he ended up on the streets, using drugs and everything else for many years. His problems eventually led to him divorcing his wife and leaving his family. One day Michael found him wandering the streets and brought him to the Church. Bernard needed much help in order to overcome his problems. He had some tough times and some hard struggles in our men's program. There were days when he wanted to return to his old habits. But, it was during one of those days that I told him, "I'll fight you, and the only way that you are going to go back is over my dead body. You will have to beat me down to go". Shortly after that, Bernard gave God his life, and allowed the Holy Spirit to take control of him. He is now saved and filled with the Holy Ghost. What we did was build Bernard up, upon the foundation of Christ. There were a number of men at Faith Clinic that we could have told Bernard to look up to, but we knew the foundation that Bernard really needed was Jesus Christ. A song writer once said, "<u>on Christ the solid rock I stand, all other ground is sinking sand</u>." Bernard is now remarried to his wife and lives in Detroit with their two children.

The true foundation

"**For other foundation can no man lay than that is laid, which is Jesus Christ . . .**" (1 Corinthians 3: 11) There is not another foundation by which men can get to God. The one and only true foundation is Jesus Christ. The choir might be world renowned, but the choir is a poor foundation. The preacher might be an excellent orator with outstanding teaching abilities, but he too is a poor foundation. We might belong to the church with the most beautiful edifice, but that edifice is a poor foundation. All of these things are wonderful in the work of God, but they are other foundations, not the foundation upon which people can build their salvation around or on. When we build on Jesus, we have His assurance that He will never leave us or fail us.

Like Michael, Bernard was built upon that solid foundation which is Jesus Christ. Both men had to be taught and did learn how to walk with the Lord. They had to develop a relationship with God for themselves. We were responsible for teaching and guiding them as they grew to know the Lord. We watched them as they practiced the word of God in their lives. We watched as they stood on the word of God for doors to open and for the favor of God to be upon their lives. They have weathered many storms, and are still standing on the true foundation, which is Jesus Christ.

Men can only experience true change in Christ

It is only in Christ that we have assurance of a new beginning and eternal life. For the scripture states, **"Therefore, if any man be in Christ, he is a new creature, behold, old things are passed away, and behold all things are become new."** (**2 Corinthians 5:17**) When they accepted Christ, Michael and Bernard were rescued from quicksand. These brothers were sinking fast, never to rise any more. But their lives were transformed; they became new creations in Christ Jesus. Their old lives literally passed away. If you knew them back then, and were to see them now, it would blow your mind! These men live productive lives; they have families, homes, automobiles, and own their own businesses. They are responsible and accountable men in their homes, community and church. For Michael and Bernard, all things have become new. These brothers have changed from the inside out. They don't talk like they used to talk and they don't spend their time at their former hangouts. They chose to build their lives on that solid foundation which is Jesus Christ our Lord.

It only takes one

Today Michael and Bernard are in ministry and they are winning men for Christ throughout Detroit. It started with one person who knew Jesus Christ. That one person found Michael and brought him to Jesus. Michael then found Bernard and brought him also to

Jesus. Now they are all building on the foundation of Christ. I wonder who you will find and bring to the Lord. Somebody is waiting on your invitation to come into the kingdom of God. They desperately need to be changed in order to become a new creature in Christ. They want to escape from being bound to sin. They want to experience life upon the Solid Rock, which is Christ Jesus.

There is no better place to build upon than the foundation of Jesus Christ. We can build our lives upon him, we can build our hopes upon him, and we can build our desires upon him. He is not going anywhere, His foundation is solid, and it is a rock.

CHAPTER III

The Right Equipment for the Job

Often we see in the news, calamities that happen in developing countries, such as earthquakes and mudslides, which destroy entire communities. One of the things that is often noticeably absent in rescue efforts, is the proper equipment. Lack of the proper equipment for any task may cause loss of productivity, injury or death. It is imperative that we have the proper equipment to get the job done in a timely manner. Every professional has tools for his/her trade, some more apparent than others. Even so, every believer has to be equipped with the right tools to bring men into the kingdom of God.

Some of the Necessary Tools

In **Colossians 3:12**, the bible instructs us to, **"Put on therefore, as the elect of God, holy and beloved bowels of mercies, kindness, humbleness of mind, meekness, longsuffering.** Here, we see God is giving us some equipment needed to do our job. This job does not require a degree in any field to be effective in bringing men to Jesus Christ. It does, however, require the right tools. Here are a few essential tools that our job requires. **The first tool** that we are admonished to possess as the elect of God, is <u>holy beloved bowels of mercies.</u> If we do not have bowels of mercies, we will not be moved to find others to bring into the kingdom of God. We will not go and get our loved ones, our neighbors, our friends our co-workers.

The second tool that we must possess is <u>kindness</u>. Sometimes there are individuals that go out to get others to come to Jesus, but they are not kind in their approach, and the way they entreat others causes people to be wounded or turned off for life.

The third tool that a person must have is <u>humbleness</u>. A person who has humbleness of mind does not think that he is any better than the person he is inviting to come to Jesus. A lack of humility causes us to behave arrogantly towards those who don't know Christ, especially if they are in a position of need.

The fourth tool that we must possess is <u>meekness</u>. Some believers confuse being meek with speaking softly. However, being meek is not being strong willed or violent, but submissive. Jesus said to His disciples as he sent them out to witness in **Matthew 10:16, ". . . be ye therefore wise as serpents, and harmless as doves.**" A person with a meek spirit will submit himself to the person to which he is witnessing. They will take time to listen to what the other person has to say, even though they may not agree. They will always respond with respect, even when the other person is disrespecting them.

The fifth tool is <u>longsuffering</u>. A person that has meekness will also be longsuffering. They will go the extra mile with the individual to whom they are witnessing. They will continue to witness to that individual when others have given up because they understand that people don't always come to Christ within the same time frame that others think they should.

These are some of our tools of the trade, and without the right tools, we will mess things up. Even though our intentions may be good, the damage that is done to a person because we are not properly equipped can be devastating. The same way we would like someone to suffer long with us, in like manner, we have to be longsuffering with others. Now, these are not the only set of tools, or pieces of equipment that you will need to get the job done. Remember, the pieces of equipment that you will need for the job will change from person to person. Everyone's problems are not the same and each problem requires specialized equipment.

Don't be caught without the Necessary Tools

Whenever we have an electrical or plumbing problem and we call for a technician, they always show up with a truck full of tools and equipment. I believe that is the way every believer should be when we are on assignment. Everything that we need should be right there with us. We should have the fruit of the Spirit right there inside of us. "**But the fruit of the Spirit is love, joy, peace, longsuffering, gentleness, goodness, faith. (23) Meekness, temperance: against such there is no law.**" (**Galatians 5:22-23**) If we don't have peace with us, we may end up in a fight, verbally or physically. If we forget to load up on love, someone may make us mad, and we might start disliking that individual. Next thing we know, there is a root of bitterness inside of us. We must have joy, no ifs, ands or buts about it. No joy, no strength; without it we are cooked. The word of God says, **"Finally, my brethren, be strong in the Lord, and in the power of His might. (11) Put on the whole armor of God, that ye may be able to stand against the wiles of the devil. (12) For we wrestle not against flesh and blood, but against principalities, against powers, against the rulers of the darkness of this world, against spiritual wickedness in high places."** **(Ephesians 6: 10-12)** A spiritual person is a well-equipped individual, and he is prepared for anything. He does not leave behind or lend any of his tools or equipment. He is charged according to **Ephesians 6:13,** " **Wherefore take unto you the whole armor of God, that ye may be able to withstand in the evil day, having done all to stand."** We have to be fully clothed, with all the applicable tools and equipment for the job at hand. There is a lot to put on, and the more we put on, the more effective we become as workers with God.

Possessing Necessary tools help us to withstand attacks

Besides being able to get the job done, we have to be able to stand in the evil day. That is the day when we come under attack from the enemy. However, after doing everything we know to do to stand, **Ephesians 6: 14-18** says, "**Stand therefore, having your loins girt about with truth, and having on the breastplate of righteousness;** (15) **And your feet shod with the preparation of the gospel of peace;** (16) **Above all, taking the shield of faith, wherewith ye shall be able to quench all the fiery darts of the wicked.** (17) **And take the helmet of salvation, and the sword of the Spirit, which is the word of God.** (18) **Praying always with all prayer and supplication in the Spirit, and watching thereunto with all perseverance and supplication for all saints.**"

Yes, We Can Win Men For Christ / Zachary N. Hicks

Having the right equipment is necessary for our spiritual survival and the survival of other saints. When the United States Military is preparing to go to war, the first thing that it does is issue hardware to the troops. These men and women have to validate that their equipment is in working condition before they get to the battlefield. Consequently, when surrounded by enemy fire, having a faulty weapon can result in unnecessary casualties or fatalities. Thus, every soldier has to check his equipment daily in order to verify that he has all his equipment and that it is in working condition. I wonder, have you checked to see if you have all your equipment, and is it in working condition, soldier? Don't take anything for granted. Stop and take inventory today.

Yes, We Can Win Men For Christ / Zachary N. Hicks

CHAPTER IV

Love Constrains Us to Pray and Act

"**Beloved, let us love one another; for love is of God, and everyone that loveth is born of God, and knoweth God.**" (**1 John 4: 7**) Every believer is known by one attribute, that is <u>love</u>. We are told to love one another, and the reason that we should love. Because everyone that loves or demonstrates love is born of God and knows God. Love is absolutely essential in a believer's life. "**He that loveth not knoweth not God, for God is love.**" (**1 John 4: 8**)

Every ministry gift, every piece of spiritual tool and equipment has to be encapsulated in love. Whatever we do towards anyone should be done with love. It does not matter what they have done to us. It is our responsibility to always entreat a person with love. We overcome evil with good, and it is good to love. "**Hatred stirreth up**

strifes, but love covereth all sins." (**Proverb 10: 12**) We don't practice sin, but we all have faults or imperfection in our lives, such as attitudes or mannerism flaws that may cause others to be offended. We have personality clashes simply because we are unique. There is not another person like us; each one of us is an original. As a result, love becomes the lubricant that keeps things smooth between us. Without this vital ingredient in our lives, we will destroy one another.

The love we are referring to is not our own ability to love, but <u>agape love.</u> Agape love is defined as unconditional love that comes from God. This is the love that God gives us, which gives us the ability to look beyond a person's faults. **Roman 5:8** states, "**But God commendeth His love towards us, in that, while we were yet sinners, Christ died for us.**" The Father loves us so much that even though we have shortcomings, He yet wants to be in relationship with MAN.

<u>We cannot win others to Christ without love</u>

Joseph was an older gentleman, and he carried himself in a stately manner. He was a man who stood out in a crowd. When Joseph first came to the church I noticed him immediately. Soon I got the opportunity to talk with him and came to know him as a pleasant and personable gentleman. I learned that prior to coming to Faith Clinic, Joseph had not attended church for more than ten years. Joseph's reason for staying away from church was that someone at the church had offended him. The person never came to Joseph in order to set things straight, and Joseph never went to the person. Further, Joseph did not pray about the matter nor did he seek the counsel of another brother. Joseph came to the conclusion that he had enough of Church and that was "the straw that broke the camel's back."

The enemy often takes advantage of our differences and disagreements. He plays it up in our minds to the extent that a molehill becomes a mountain. Barriers are quickly erected, lines are drawn in the sand, and sides are taken. That is the way the enemy wants us to behave; that is the mindset of the world. But that is not the way we have learned to behave in Christ. It is imperative that after we get saved, we do not continue to conform to the thinking of the world. We have to renew our minds with the word of God, which brings about a transformation in the way we think. Whether we are the offender or the offended; when armed with love and a renewed mind, we know how to deal with our molehills. "**And above all things have fervent charity among yourselves; for charity shall cover a multitude of sins.**" (**1 Peter 4: 8**) This is the approach we took with Joseph. We loved him and loved him some more. We taught Joseph to keep his eyes on Christ by answering his questions and pointing him to God's word. With time Joseph became very faithful in the ministry, and worked hard witnessing and caring for others until the Lord called him home. Without agape love, we could not have won Joseph to Christ.

Love and prayer

With agape love, we can rescue our sons and daughters from the streets or adultery and fornication, and bring them to Jesus. We may not be able to bring them physically today, but every day we can

Yes, We Can Win Men For Christ / Zachary N. Hicks

bring them in prayer. "**For the love of Christ constrains us...**" (2 Corinthians 5: 14), and "**Knowing therefore the terror of the Lord, we persuade men...**" (2 Corinthians 5:11) Love will cause us to pray and act, for the scripture states; "**For God so loved the world, that he gave His only begotten son, that whosoever believeth in Him should not perish, but have everlasting life.**" (St. John 3: 16) The world needs to experience God's love, and the way for this to happen, is for every believer to go and get someone and bring that person to Jesus. Let's keep doing this over and over and over again. There are teachers, doctors, magistrates, politicians, business people, civil service workers, et cetera, that are waiting on an invitation just from us to come to Jesus.

David was a Track Coach at Tougaloo College, outside of Jackson, Mississippi, when he received his invitation to come to Jesus. He often testifies that he is so thankful that a freshman in college by the name of Angela, had the audacity to stand up and tell him the truth about salvation. David wanted to be saved, but was unsure what his next step should be. As a result, upon being introduced to Jesus Christ, David decided to become one of His followers. Today, David is no longer coaching track, but he is coaching men through his teachings, encouraging them to come and meet Jesus.

"**By this shall all men know that ye are my disciples, if ye have love one to another.**" (**St. John 13: 35**) Our love for one another is an outward sign to the world that we are true followers of Jesus Christ. It is by this demonstration of our love that we can pull men out of the world and into the kingdom of God. Our love is vibrant, pure, and has the power to change those that come into contact with it. This love not only constrains us to act and pray, it compels us to show mercy, forgive, reconcile, and to be longsuffering with all men. No wonder it is often sung about and referred to as "such wondrous love" and "no greater love". <u>For this love is God's love and it has the power to change men's lives, if we will only share it</u>!!!

After all, love is what most people are looking for. We were once just like them, in the world, looking for love in all the wrong places.

We thought we could find love in a man or a woman. After we got them however, we were still not satisfied. We thought if we drank, partied and stayed out all night, we would find love, but love always seemed to evade us. We never realized that we were looking for love in the wrong place, until someone invited us to come to Jesus. And now we have found that all we need is His love.

Yes, We Can Win Men For Christ / Zachary N. Hicks

CHAPTER V

Reaping Your Harvest

Then said Jesus unto His disciples, "**The *harvest* truly is plenteous, but the laborers are few, pray ye therefore the Lord of the harvest, that he will send forth laborers into His harvest.**" **(Matthew 9: 37-38)** The time to harvest the world is now. Men desperately need to be introduced to Jesus. Everywhere you look, you can see men that are ripe and ready to be picked for the Lord. In fact, ever since Jesus made this statement to His disciples, we have been experiencing a bumper crop harvest. The problem is, there are not enough laborers to work the harvest. Every year the fruit falls to the ground and dies by the thousand before anyone can get to it.

Go into the harvest

This does not have to be the case in our personal ministry. We can go into the harvest and reap our harvest of men for the Lord. This does not mean that once we win a certain number of men that we should stop. It is my belief that we can reach everyone that God has ordained from the beginning of the world for us to reach. We never have to give up on our loved ones or anyone for that matter. Through loving kindness, longsuffering, and patience we can ultimately bring people to Jesus Christ. Bringing men to Jesus Christ is not easy, but it can be done. With every person that we extend an invitation to come to Jesus, comes a unique set of challenges for us to help them get through. Some are more complex than others and they require more sacrifice on our part than others. For some, we may have to commit many days of prayer and fasting for their deliverance, before they can begin to look toward the Lord. **"Howbeit this kind goeth not out but by prayer and fasting." (Matthew 17:21)**

Whatever their hang-ups may be, we need not despair. We are not in this by ourselves. We always have help. We are working together with God. In **Zechariah 4:6** the Bible states, **". . .This is the word of the Lord unto Zerubbabel, saying, Not by might, nor by** power, but by my Spirit, saith the Lord of hosts."** God anointed Zerubbabel to accomplish the task that was set before him. Similarly, God will anoint us to win souls for His kingdom, if we will go into the harvest.

Sometimes bringing individuals to Christ becomes very personal for us. They may be a loved one, a close friend, or even part of our inner circle. As a result, we make their struggle our struggle and their pain becomes our pain. Soon this person can become a weight that is pulling us down both physically and spiritually. The key to reaping, if there is a key, is to have faith in God and to remain focused on Him. **"For we walk by faith, not by sight"** (2 **Corinthians 5:7**)

We can't do it, but God can

2 **Chronicles 20: 15** states, "**... for the battle is not yours, but God's.**" This is God's harvest, we are just laborers in His harvest. If problems arise, and the person seems to be getting worse instead of better, don't fret or fuss with them. **1 Peter 5: 7** says, "**Casting all**

your care upon Him, for He careth for you." Believe me, Jesus cares about His workers. He never leaves us to bear things alone, but we have to continuously cast all our cares upon Him. I am not saying that you will not shed some tears at times, or in your secret closet. However, we have scriptures and the Holy Ghost to encourage and comfort us. **Hebrews 13:5** states, "**. . . I will never leave thee, nor forsake thee.**" We know whose report we believe. We believe the report of the Lord. "**. . . for as soon as Zion travailed, she brought forth her children.**" **(Isaiah 66:8)** Sometimes we may have to travail in order to birth that soul that is poised to come forth, but is hindered for whatever reason.

If we stay focused and have faith in God, we shall reap if we don't faint. "**Be not deceived; God is not mocked: for whatsoever a man soweth, that shall he also reap.**" **(Galatians 6:7)** This is wonderful news. If we labor in God's harvest, we most certainly shall reap from His harvest. Don't let anyone deceive you. God is not a man who tells lies. If you work, you will get paid. God is bound by

His word.

Sister Debra had a brother in jail. For years, she kept praying for him and believing God for his release and salvation. During tough times she would ask the church to pray for her brother. Regardless of the opposition, and the ups and downs, she never gave up. Today her brother, **Norris**, is out of jail. Debra brought Norris to Jesus, and he is now preaching and has a wonderful wife.

My friend, you also can reap your harvest. Have faith in God, stay focused, and soon your loved ones and those in your inner circle will be following Jesus with you. **"And let us not be weary in well doing; for in due season we shall reap, if we faint not." (Galatians 6:9)** Remember, our season is assured if we don't quit.

Carl, my biological brother, is a prime example of why we should never give up on anyone. We were raised in a Christian home. Our father was a preacher and our mother was a prayer warrior. However, as a teenager, Carl chose the way of the world. He did everything from using hard drugs, selling drugs, committing armed robbery, to almost anything else that you could imagine. For almost thirty years Carl stayed in the world, but we never gave up on him. My parents prayed and fasted for him, and loved him. After my father made his transition from labor to reward, my mother, sisters and I continued to fight for Carl's soul. (My father, Superintendent Edgar Hicks passed in 1987) Finally, after almost thirty years in the clutches of the enemy, Carl came to Jesus. My mother lived to see Carl come to Jesus. Today he is an Associate Pastor, a family man, and is winning men to Christ. Remember, we shall reap if we don't quit.

CHAPTER VI

Renewing the Minds of Men

It is often stated that the mind is the devil's battleground. Perhaps, it is based on the scripture in **Ephesians 6: 12,** which says, **"For we wrestle not against flesh and blood, but against principalities, against powers, against the rulers of the darkness of this world, against spiritual wickedness in high places."** I believe that the devil works on men overtime, since God made man the head of the woman and of the home. Often, our battle with the enemy as new believers takes place in the mind. It is in the mind that men struggle with pornography, sexual addictions, evil thoughts, and ungodliness. As babes in Christ the enemy bombards us with all of our former lusts and desires. He holds nothing back, pulls no punches, and all he wants is to kill our relationship with God.

He works methodically and tirelessly to accomplish his

mission. He will use and send you the best under his command to cause you to abort your decision to follow Jesus. There are times shortly after one has been saved, when it may seem like the best of everything is passing you by. For example, if you previously enjoyed sleeping with different partners, after you are saved it may seem like the cream of the crop comes knocking at your door. Perhaps, it was a drug addiction you struggled to maintain, and it ruined your health, your life and your finances. Now that you are saved, the enemy is sending old friends by that are offering the drugs to you for free. It never bothered you before you got saved to lie to better yourself in life. However, since you've been saved you have been offered a promotion, an opportunity of a lifetime. You know that you are not qualified for this promotion, and if you were to apply it would require you to lie on the application and your resume. These are just a few ways the enemy tries every new believer. He keeps flooding our minds with sensual desires, things that the flesh craves. He makes it so much more attractive and appealing to the eyes, that if we are not careful we will take the bait. Remember, the enemy tempted Jesus three times, and in the third temptation, he showed Him all the kingdoms of the world and offered Him all the power and glory. We should take the instruction given by Jesus in his response to the enemy's temptation, "**get thee hence Satan**". **(Matthew 4:1-11)**

God's word renews the mind

For us to respond like Christ we have to renew our minds. **Romans 12: 2** says "**And be not conformed to this world; but be ye transformed by the renewing of your mind, that ye may prove what is that good, and acceptable, and perfect, will of God.**" Before we got saved, our minds were conformed to this world. For a transformation to occur, our minds need to be renewed. <u>The word of God is absolutely essential in renewing man's mind</u>. When man <u>accepts</u> and <u>obeys</u> God's word, his mind is renewed. This is how we prove what is that good, and acceptable, and perfect will of God. <u>The more of God's word we accept and obey; the more we put on the mind of Christ</u>. "A tooth for a tooth, and an eye for an eye" was how we used to think, but not anymore. That was before we knew Christ and started living by His every word.

The word tells us, **"Let this mind be in you, which was also in Christ Jesus."** (**Philippians 2:5**) It is through the word that we learn the mindset of Jesus Christ. We never do anything for strife or vain glory. With humility, we esteem others higher than ourselves, never looking upon our own abilities or accomplishments, but upon others around us. When our mind has been renewed, we never boast about ourselves. We are no longer seeking the praises of men, but our intent is for God to get the glory in our lives.

The word must be obeyed

Change sometimes is not easy. However, if we are going to become more like Christ we have to feast on His word daily. That is how we avoid falling into sin, because the scripture states**, Psalm 119:11**, "**Thy word have I hid in my heart, that I might not sin against thee.**" The more word we receive and hide inside of us, the less chance of us sinning against God. "**Thy word is a lamp unto my

feet, and a light unto my path". (**Psalm 119:105**) The word will become a lamp to our feet, showing to us where we are stepping, and a light that lights our path before us. Many have erred due to the fact that they have failed to get into the word of God, while others failed because they did not allow the word to really get inside of them.

    Barry was a young man that came to Faith Clinic for help. He was addicted to crack cocaine, and was literally on the run for his life. He was very bright, analytical, astute, and well versed in the scriptures. The first time at our Ministry House program, Barry failed. In fact, with all of his scriptural knowledge Barry not only failed one time, but three times. He knew the word, but had not committed himself to <u>obeying the word.</u> It was not hidden in his heart. It was in his memory, but not in his heart. Some within the ministry began to give up on Barry and didn't think he was serious, or wanted any help, and wrote him off. However, Barry came back a fourth time, and on his fourth attempt, he yielded himself to Christ. Barry began to obey the word of God and his mindset began to change. **"Wherewithal**

shall a young man cleanse his way? By taking heed thereto according to thy word." **(Psalm 119: 9)** The word if applied and obeyed has the power to renew minds and clean a man up. Barry is now preaching God's word and encouraging other men to enhance their relationship with Christ. God has also blessed him with a wife.

Once a man's mind has been renewed, he can make it in Jesus Christ. It does not mean that he knows everything or has a perfect understanding of Christ; it simply means that he has chosen to be a follower and to learn of Him. In **Matthew 11: 29**, Jesus said, "**Take my yoke upon you and learn of me, ...** (30) **For my yoke is easy and my burden is light**." One has to learn about Christ first, before he can begin to walk and talk like Him. One has to study His life, His ministry, get to know his passion and mindset, and allow the word to transform him day by day.

CHAPTER VII

Nurturing Spiritual Babies, But Men

When we first get saved, we all need to be nurtured and mentored. It does not matter how old we are, what our worldly qualifications are, and how much wealth we possess. This is a very important step in our spiritual growth, without it many will make a mess of their spiritual lives. For most of us, we had someone in the church that took us under their wings and helped us overcome our growing pains. Most of the time, when we get hired for a job, we are placed with someone who will teach us the ins and outs of the company. Even so in Christ; Paul says, "**Now I say, that the heir, as long as he is a child, differs nothing from a servant, though he be lord of all**; (2) **But is under tutors and governors until the time appointed of the Father.**" (Galatians 4: 1-2)

New believers must be mentored

New believers, most certainly are appointed by the Father to be under tutors and governors. God gives each of us a person or persons that He has prepared to deal with us. They know how to wait on babes in Christ. They are mature and seasoned, not novices in the things of God. It is God that guides both parties and brings them together. Without realizing it, a bond quickly develops between a babe in Christ and the mentor. Like a natural parent, the spiritual parent nurtures and guides the child until it is grown. Often this nurturing is complicated by the fact that we are nurturing adults; people that have families, own businesses, are head of corporations, hold multiple degrees, and are well established in the community. Nevertheless, this God-given process has to continue within the body. Whenever this process is circumvented to accommodate any person, that person's spiritual life is sabotaged.

<u>We need spiritual parents to train us, rebuke and chasten us when we are wrong</u>. We also need spiritual parents to love and

embrace us and encourage us to be strong. They will pray for us when most others stop. They are appointed by God to bring us to maturity. Paul said about Timothy in **Philippians 2: 20-21**, "**For I have no man likeminded, who will naturally care for your state.** (21) **For all seek their own, not the things which are Jesus Christ's.**" Those that God appoints to nurture us never seek their own interest. They always seek the things of Jesus Christ for our lives.

The importance of a God given mentor

David was twenty-seven years old when he met **Mother Josephine**, who was eighty years old. He had just joined the church and given his life to God. Shortly after joining the church, Mother Josephine asked David to give her a ride home from church. After giving her a ride, she asked him if he could take her to the store the following day. The next day, after taking her to the store, she invited him into her home. Over the years, until her death at age ninety-six, Mother Josephine was David's spiritual mother. She saw things in him that he never knew were there; she believed in him and kept nudging him more and more towards the deeper things of God. Mother Josephine had an excellent spirit; she was gentle, patient and kind. She was a woman of few words, with the gift of discernment. God used her to nurture many sons and daughters in the gospel. It was her temperament and love for Christ, and the daily reminders to "stay with God" that helped David in those formative years. Mother Josephine went home to be with the Lord in 2003. Sixteen years after they met, some of the things that Mother Josephine spoke into David's life are coming to pass.

I am so glad that Jesus did not leave us to raise ourselves. He gave us people who know how to entreat us; they are tough when they have to be tough and gentle too. **"But we were gentle among you, even as a nurse cherishes her children**; (8) **So being affectionately desirous of you, we were willing to have imparted unto you, not the gospel of God only, but our own souls, because ye were dear unto us." (1 Thessalonians 2: 7-8)** This woman cherished David as one of her children, and imparted not just the gospel of Jesus Christ, but her spirit of grace, mercy and love into his life. Mother Josephine understood her assignment and her responsibility, and knew how to treat the children that God gave her to nurture. They were grown men and women, but they were her spiritual children. We can all borrow a page from Mother Josephine, as God brings men into our life to be cared for, loved and nurtured. We must be led by God and know when to be tough and gentle.

Yes, We Can Win Men For Christ / Zachary N. Hicks

CHAPTER VIII

Preparing Men for the Harvest

The cycle of sowing and reaping has been going on ever since the beginning of the world. As a matter of fact, everything that is living has a reproductive cycle. The bible states in **Ecclesiastes 3: 1-2**, "**To everything there is a season, and a time to every purpose under heaven**; (2) **A time to be born, and a time to die; a time to plant, and a time to pluck up that which is planted.**" Whenever the reproductive cycle of life stops, life will eventually cease.

The cycle of sowing and reaping in the kingdom of God has to continue. The older saints are being called home from their labor, and fresh laborers are needed to fill their ranks. This process requires us to pray always for God to send laborers into His harvest. We have a great responsibility to prepare those men and women that God has entrusted into our care. The task is not a simple one, but under the

Master's leadership we can do all things. (**Philippians 4:13**)

Winning men to Christ requires faithfulness to the task

God is looking for faithful men. He wants to know who is willing and ready to go on His behalf. **Isaiah 6:8** states, "**Also I heard the voice of the Lord, saying, whom shall I send, and who will go for us? Then said I, here am I, send me.**" Isaiah's iniquity was taken away and his sins purged when one of the Seraphims touched his lips with a piece of hot coal from the altar. Immediately, he heard the voice of the Lord asking whom shall He send? Isaiah's response was here I am, I am saved Lord, my sins and iniquity you have taken away. Send me Lord, I will go. When God cleans us up, we are ready to go. However, we must submit ourselves to the tutors, spiritual parents, and the pastors that God has placed us under so that they can do the job of nurturing, and admonishing us in the things of God, that we will be thoroughly furnished unto every good work. It is not God's will for his laborers to be ill equipped. "**Study to shew thyself approved unto God, a workman that needeth not to be**

ashamed, rightly dividing the word of truth." (**2 Timothy 2:15**) Before we go into the harvest, we should have invested a considerable amount of time in prayer, fasting and the study of God's word.

Paul was a man that responded like Isaiah when he met the Lord. He was threatening to slaughter the disciples of the Lord and had obtained letters permitting him to go to Damascus, and if he found any followers of Christ there, that he could bring them bound, back to Jerusalem. "**And he fell to the earth, and heard a voice saying unto him, Saul, Saul, why persecutest thou me?** (5) **And he said, who art thou, Lord? And the Lord said, I am Jesus whom thou persecutest; it is hard to kick against the pricks.** (6) **And he trembling and astonished said, Lord, what will you have me to do? And the Lord said unto him; Arise, and go into the city, and it shall be told thee what thou must do.**" (**Acts 9: 4-6**)

Lord what will you have me to do?

Paul's encounter with Jesus changed his life forever. Paul's life was changed to the point that his response to the Lord was, **Lord what** will you have me to do? The scripture declares that Paul was with the disciples at Damascus certain days. For a certain number of days Paul spent under tutors. Ananias and other disciples taught him about Jesus Christ being the Son of God. After meeting the Lord in the way, and then having the scriptures about Christ explained to him more clearly, Paul was ready to go out and preach. **"And when he had received meat, he was strengthen. Then was Saul (Paul) certain days with the disciples, which were at Damascus.** (20) **And straightway he preached Christ in the synagogues, that He is the Son of God."** (**Acts 9:19-20**) When God shows us mercy and changes our lives, we, like Paul, should respond by saying, Lord what will you have me to do?

CHAPTER IX

Men that Overcame

Hebrews 11:4-39, shares with us the testimonies of those that trusted in God. Men such as Abel, Enoch, Noah, Abraham, Isaac, Joseph, and Moses' parents are just a few of the individuals highlighted in scriptures. All of these individuals overcame through faith in God.

As in times past, even so today, the enemy is working on causing our downfall. Today we can declare with triumph "**And they overcame him by the blood of the Lamb, and the word of their testimony; and they loved not their lives unto death.**" (**Revelation 12:11**) Christ has used us to help many men overcome their situation, and come to know Him as their Lord and Savior. Here are a few testimonies of additional men that we labored with and who came to know the Lord in the pardon of their sins, and who are now winning other men to Christ. They are sons and brothers, fathers and husbands, and grandfathers and uncles. Join us, and the number can increase ten thousand percent.

James is a tremendous man of God, but he did not start out that way. One night he was attacked by some men, and was beaten and left for dead on a darkened street corner. He was not saved, and his lifestyle (of drug addiction, alcoholism, and selling drugs, etc.,) had caught up with him. However, he had a wife that believed God for his salvation. **Sister Beulah** prayed for her husband, and while he layed beaten on that darkened street corner, God preserved his life and did not suffer him to be run over by an automobile. He was discovered the next morning severely beaten and in need of immediate medical attention. Because his wife did not give up on him, today he is saved and an Associate Pastor. His wife is an Evangelist and they have a beautiful family.

Shawn was never involved with drugs. He works in Corporate America and has a beautiful family. He came to Faith Clinic looking for truth and wanting to get closer to Jesus. Shawn had been hurt in another ministry, due to some erroneous biblical teaching. We put our arms around him, loved him, taught him more of the word of God and helped keep his eyes on Christ. Today he is a deacon. He and his wife are doing a wonderful work within our ministry. God has blessed them with a beautiful son also.

Charles is another example of why we should never give up on men. When we first met several years ago, I found out that he had traveled extensively and had overcome some tough times in his life. However, he had never made a true commitment to be at any one church. In fact, Charles never attended the same church more than four weeks in a row. When he joined Faith Clinic, he was determined to make a change. He struggled and was discouraged at times, but we were determined not to give up on him. His wife and I continued to encourage him and today, he is faithful to the ministry. He is a deacon and a tremendous help to others, and also has a beautiful family.

Gary had a history of drug abuse. He was street-wise and did not trust anyone when he first came to the ministry. He was quiet, introverted, and preferred not to socialize. He appeared hard and cold to others. We began to love him and gave him plenty of attention. We gave him the word and supported him when he did not understand. Little by little, his demeanor began to soften. He began to mingle among others more, as his confidence grew. Today he is a deacon with a beautiful wife and they are both faithful to ministry.

Wilfred was a family man who was unemployed, on public assistance, and without an automobile. To add to his problems, he was an alcoholic. We began to minister to Wilfred regularly, embracing and loving him. We shared the word of God with him, and we were longsuffering until we were able to lead him to Christ. Today he is an Associate Pastor and very faithful to the Lord with a wonderful family. He is also the leader of our Men's Ministry.

Fernando is a very talented young man. When we first met many years ago, his thinking was way off. He was a very successful musician playing for other churches. He was involved in gang activities, the selling of large quantities of drugs, shootouts, and much more. When you were around him, you were literally taking your life into your own hands, because so many people wanted to see him dead. He used to justify his lifestyle with incorrect application of the Word of God. The environment in which he lived had shaped his mindset, and at times he did not rightly divide the word of truth. Working with Fernando was not easy, he tested our love for him. We had to be very, very long longsuffering, and patient. Many times he came short, but we continued to pray for him and love him. We shared the word and kept on trying to point him to Christ. It took several years, and many tears, but we had faith in God, and believed God in spite of how he acted. One day Fernando gave his life to God, totally surrendering to the will of God. Now he is preaching God's word and using his many musical talents to the glory of God.

These represent just a fraction of the many testimonies that Christ has brought forth. As you continue to witness and/or mentor, remember, God can do anything, except fail.

Yes, We Can Win Men For Christ / Zachary N. Hicks

CHAPTER X

Summary

"Can we win men for Christ? Yes, we can. When God spoke to Abraham about the birth of a son Isaac in his old age, He said, "**Is there anything too hard for the Lord? . . .**" **(Genesis 18:14)** Again, He spoke through Peter assuring us that (He) "**is not willing that any should perish, but that all should come to repentance.**" **(2 Peter 3:9)**

I ask you, <u>if not now, when?</u> <u>If not you and I, who?</u> The harvest truly is ripe, but the laborers are few. For far too long we have been at a standstill, partially because we have felt unprepared and ill equipped for the job. Many felt they were not called to the work, but every born again believer has a testimony to give. That testimony is a witness of the grace and power of God.

Many often say they don't have the ability, but <u>if we make</u>

ourselves available to God, through Jesus Christ and the working of the Holy Ghost, He will call us into the vineyard to work. I believe it!!! This is the eleventh hour and the harvest is ripe. Let us gird up the loins of our mind, prepare ourselves mentally, spiritually and physically to reap the harvest. The saints used to sing a song: "bringing in the sheaves, bringing in the sheaves, we shall come rejoicing, bringing in the sheaves." What a wonderful day to appear before the Lord with fruit won through our testimonies, our love of God, our longsuffering and kindness!!! Men are searching for something and someone worth living for. We have the answer. He is Jesus Christ, the Son of the Living God.

We are called to expand the family of God, to get ourselves, brothers and sisters in Christ. He commanded us to "**. . . go therefore out into the highways and hedges, and compel them to come in, that my house might be filled.**" (**Luke 14:23**) Since we are co-laborers with God in this work, we cannot fail. The early and the latter rain are necessary to bring in the harvest. The scripture exhorts and encourages us to "**Be not weary in well doing, for in due season we shall reap, if we faint not.**" **(Galatians 6:9)**

Isaiah 12:3 says, "**Therefore with joy shall ye draw water out of the wells of salvation.**" For some time I have thought that this was just for me; that we each draw water out of our own wells. Now, when I consider this scripture, I envision someone pulling up water out of the well of salvation, and giving it to the people around them who are dying of thirst, <u>so they can live</u>.

Sharing that life-giving water with those who are dying brings joy to the one who is drawing the water to distribute it!!! That's you and I, my brothers and sisters. There is joy for us who will share the life-giving waters of salvation.

There is no doubt ... YES, WE CAN WIN MEN FOR CHRIST.

Notes

NOTES

NOTES

NOTES

NOTES

NOTES

About the Author

Pastor Zachary N, Hicks was born and raised in Detroit, Michigan. After suffering a serious burn to his right leg at age 4, doctors said "he will never walk again and certainly will not be able to run and jump like other kids." However, God completely healed him. He went on to graduate from Detroit's Southeastern High School and to have a successful collegiate and post collegiate basketball career. He graduated from Northern Michigan University in Marquette, Michigan, with a Bachelor of Science degree.

In November of 1991, Bishop P. A. Brooks recognized that Pastor Hicks was saved, full of the Holy Ghost and had accepted his calling. Bishop Brooks then appointed Pastor Hicks as the pastor of Faith Clinic Church Of God In Christ in Detroit, Michigan. Starting with approximately 20 members, at the printing of this book God has blessed him to now pastor over 2800 people and the ministry continues to grow rapidly.

God has given Pastor Hicks such a tremendous gift to minister to men from all walks of life. He and his wife Lisa are the founders of the Love Outreach Service Center (a residential setting that houses single men and men with children), Men Ministering To Men Ministry, Saving Empty Rare Vessels Everywhere Ministry, as well as a number of other ministries. God has used these ministries to literally win thousand of men for the body of Christ. Pastor Hicks is an author, teacher, revivalist, and conference speaker. He can be seen and heard throughout America on the "Love Outreach Television Broadcast"

Pastor Hicks and his wife, Lisa Marie, live in Detroit, Michigan. They have four wonderful children, Zachary Jr. Terrance, Krystal and Angel.